j
577.5
Winn
Winner, Cherie
  Life in the tundra

03-457

Hagerstown-Jefferson
Township Library

LIBRARY HOURS

MON	10:30-6	THU	10:30-7:30
TUE	10:30-7:30	FRI	10:30-6
WED	10:30-2:30	SAT	10:30-2:30

RD R

LIFE IN THE
TUNDRA

LIFE IN THE TUNDRA

CHERIE WINNER

Lerner Publications Company
Minneapolis

The author thanks Dr. James Ebersole of Colorado College, Colorado Springs; and my advisers on the ground in Barrow, Alaska, Frank Willingham of Ilisagvik College, Robert Suydam of the North Slope Borough Department of Wildlife Management, and Geoff Carroll of the Alaska Department of Fish and Game, for their patience and generosity in sharing their knowledge of the North Slope.

Lerner Publications Company
A division of Lerner Publishing Group
241 First Avenue North
Minneapolis, MN 55401 U.S.A.

Website address: www.lernerbooks.com

Library of Congress Cataloging-in-Publication Data

Winner, Cherie.
    Life in the tundra / by Cherie Winner.
        p.   cm. — (Ecosystems in action)
    Summary: Examines the physical features, processes, and many different species of plants and animals that make up the ecosystem of Alaska's North Slope.
    Includes bibliographical references and index.
    ISBN: 0-8225-4686-8 (lib. bdg. : alk. paper)
    1. Tundra ecology—Alaska—North Slope—Juvenile literature. [1. Tundras. 2. Tundra ecology. 3. Ecology. 4. Alaska.] I. Title. II. Series.
QH105.A4 W56 2003
577.5'86'097987—dc21   2002012173

Manufactured in the United States of America
1 2 3 4 5 6 – JR – 08 07 06 05 04 03

CONTENTS

CHAPTER ONE
WHAT IS AN ECOSYSTEM?

Rain strikes the ground near a cottongrass plant. While the plant's roots soak up the water from the soil, a lemming nibbles on its leaves. The rain muffles the footsteps of a fox creeping toward the little rodent. In a flash, the fox pounces on the lemming and devours it.

The fox, the lemming, and the cottongrass plant, as well as the rain and the soil, are partners in an ecosystem—the network of all the living things in a specific area and all the nonliving things that support them or limit them. An ecosystem may be small, like a pond, or huge, like the Great Plains. What makes it an ecosystem is that all the organisms living there are linked through their use of energy and nutrients.

Plants and some microbes bring energy into the ecosystem through the process of photosynthesis. They use energy from the Sun and nutrients from the soil to make carbohydrates, such as sugars and starches.

Because they are the first sources of food in the ecosystem, these organisms are called primary producers. Lemmings are primary consumers, or herbivores. They eat plants, such as cottongrass, and gain the energy and nutrients stored in the plants. The energy and nutrients continue to travel through the ecosystem if another animal, such as a fox, eats the lemming. The fox is a secondary consumer, or carnivore.

Decomposers are also crucial members of every ecosystem. These organisms break down dead tissue so the nutrients can return to the soil. Animals, fungi, and bacteria may act as decomposers.

In every ecosystem, the flow of energy and nutrients depends on physical aspects of the place. If the soil is too cold or wet, decomposers work very slowly, and plants may not get enough nutrients to grow large. Physical factors such as temperature and rainfall determine what kind of ecosystem can exist in a place because they determine what organisms can survive there.

TUNDRA ECOSYSTEMS

Tundra ecosystems occur in places where the summers are too cool and too short for trees to grow. They can be found in two kinds of environments. Alpine tundra occurs on high mountains all over the world. Arctic tundra occurs in the far northern parts of North America, Europe, and Asia. Although both kinds of tundra lack trees, they differ in many ways. Alpine tundra is often rocky, steep, and dry. Most arctic tundra is flat or gently rolling land dotted with ponds, lakes, and marshes.

This book focuses on the arctic tundra of northern Alaska, a region called the North Slope. The most important physical factor on the North Slope is permafrost—ground that stays frozen all year long. Only the top several inches of soil thaw each summer. Plant roots and burrowing animals remain in this thin active layer of soil. They cannot penetrate the permafrost, which may reach 1,000 feet (300 meters) down into the earth.

Despite the hardships, this arctic tundra ecosystem teems with life. A single tundra meadow may have dozens of kinds of flowers blooming at once. Insects fill the air, and small mammals scurry along the ground. Millions of birds raise their young in the tundra's wide-open spaces. For organisms that can adapt to its challenging conditions, Alaska's North Slope tundra makes a good home.

PHYSICAL FACTORS DETERMINE WHAT KIND OF ECOSYSTEM CAN EXIST IN A PARTICULAR PLACE BECAUSE THEY DETERMINE WHAT ORGANISMS CAN SURVIVE THERE.

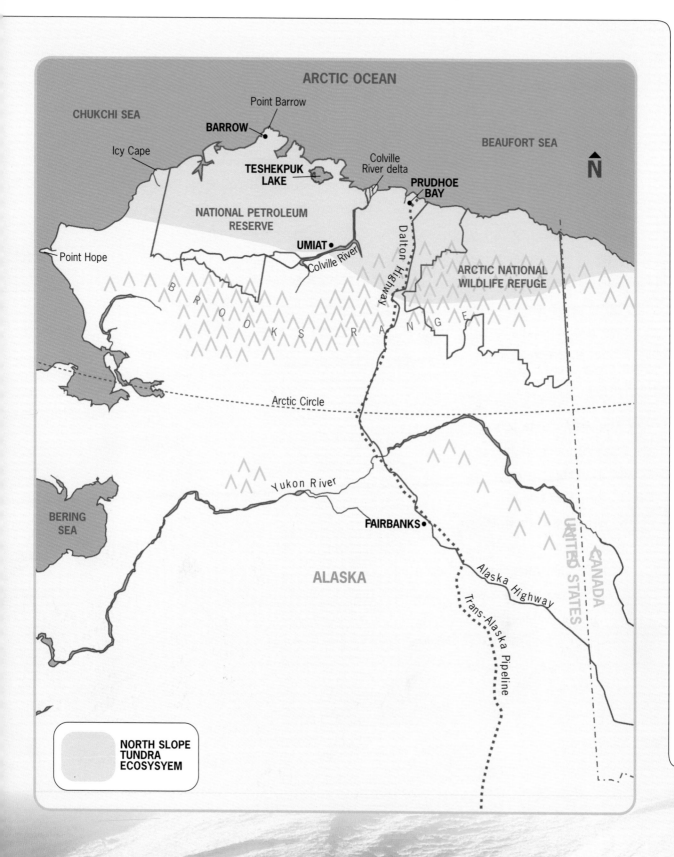

ARCTIC OCEAN

CHUKCHI SEA

BEAUFORT SEA

Point Barrow

BARROW

Icy Cape

Colville
River delta

**TESHEKPUK
LAKE**

**PRUDHOE
BAY**

NATIONAL PETROLEUM
RESERVE

Point Hope

UMIAT

Colville River

Dalton Highway

**ARCTIC NATIONAL
WILDLIFE REFUGE**

B R O O K S   R A N G E

Arctic Circle

Yukon River

BERING
SEA

FAIRBANKS

ALASKA

UNITED STATES

CANADA

Alaska Highway

Trans-Alaska Pipeline

**NORTH SLOPE
TUNDRA
ECOSYSYEM**

CHAPTER 1
ALASKA'S NORTH SLOPE TUNDRA

The North Slope's arctic tundra spans about 550 miles (890 kilometers) across northern Alaska. Along its northern border, the tundra meets the Arctic Ocean, which encircles the North Pole. Animals such as seals and whales cruise its waters. Polar bears roam the ice that covers it for several months every year. The part of the ocean that lies west of Point Barrow is called the Chukchi Sea. The part east of Point Barrow is known as the Beaufort Sea.

The North Slope ecosystem extends southward to the mountains of the Brooks Range. Along this border, it gradually gives way to two other ecosystems. In some places, it merges with alpine tundra. In other areas, the arctic tundra blends into boreal forest. Trees can grow here because the warmer, longer summers leave gaps in the permafrost, making it possible for roots to penetrate deeper into the soil.

Dozens of rivers pour out of the Brooks Range, flow across the tundra, and eventually empty into the Arctic Ocean. Every spring, these rivers rage with meltwater from mountain snow.

THE BROOKS RANGE LOOMS ABOVE ALASKA'S ARCTIC TUNDRA.

The largest is the Colville River. It flows east through the foothills before turning north across the tundra. It empties into the Beaufort Sea between Point Barrow and Prudhoe Bay.

As the Colville River nears the coast, it cuts side channels that weave around sandbars and islands. The broad area the channels cross on their way to the ocean is called a delta. Wildlife biologists call the Colville River delta and nearby Teshekpuk Lake biological hot spots because they are crucial to the survival of many of the ecosystem's animal species. At 20 miles (30 kilometers) across and 20 feet (6 meters) deep, Teshekpuk Lake is by far the largest lake in the ecosystem. In summer, thousands of caribou crowd its shores. Millions of ducks, geese, sandpipers, and other birds come to Teshekpuk Lake and the Colville River delta to find mates, make nests, and raise their young.

WILDLIFE BIOLOGISTS CALL THE COLVILLE RIVER DELTA AND NEARBY TESHEKPUK LAKE BIOLOGICAL HOT SPOTS BECAUSE THEY ARE CRUCIAL TO THE SURVIVAL OF MANY OF THE ECOSYSTEM'S ANIMAL SPECIES.

SEASONS ON THE TUNDRA

To understand why the arctic tundra is so cold, take a look at a globe. One of the first things you'll notice is that Earth is tilted. As our planet moves through space, some areas receive more hours of sunlight each day than other areas. This changes with the seasons. When the Northern Hemisphere tilts toward the Sun, it is summer in North America, Europe, and Asia and winter in South America, southern Africa, and Australia. When the Southern Hemisphere receives more sunlight, the seasons reverse. Then it is summer in the south and winter in the north.

In the Northern Hemisphere, the shortest day of the year is December 22.

We receive fewer hours of daylight on this day than on any other day of the year. But not everyone in North America receives the same amount of daylight. The farther north you are, the shorter this day is. People in New York experience fewer hours of daylight than people in Florida. In Maine, the day is even shorter.

If you study the northern part of a globe closely, you will see a line drawn around it. This represents the Arctic Circle. At any place on this line, the Sun barely shows over the horizon on December 22. North of this line—in the Arctic—the Sun doesn't rise at all on that day. The farther north of this line you go, the more days there are when the Sun doesn't rise. Instead of seeing the big, bright ball of the Sun come up, residents of the Arctic see the eastern sky brighten for a while and then go dark again.

The entire North Slope ecosystem lies more than 150 miles (240 kilometers) north of the Arctic Circle. At Barrow, the Sun doesn't rise at all from November 18 to January 24. During this time, the tundra glows with a soft dawn light for about four hours each day. The rest of the time, it huddles in darkness.

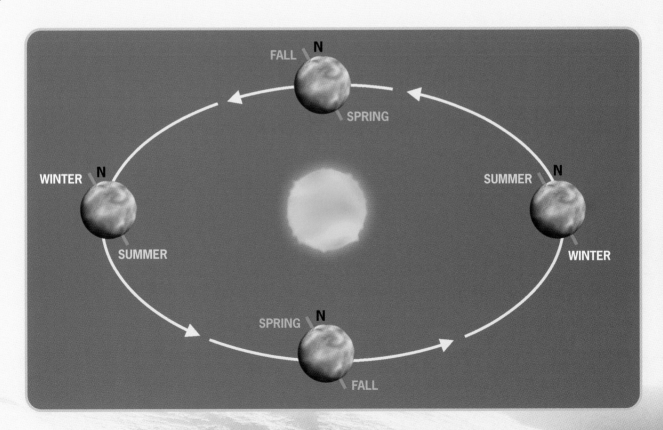

SEASONAL CYCLES IN THE NORTHERN AND SOUTHERN HEMISPHERES

As Earth continues its annual trip around the Sun, its tilt brings more light to the Northern Hemisphere again. The Sun begins to peek over the arctic horizon each morning, but it doesn't rise very high in the sky. It provides little light and heat to the frozen ground. Each day, the Sun rises a little higher in the sky, and the daylight lasts several minutes longer. Around June, the ice sheets on tundra rivers, lakes, and the ocean begin to break up into floating chunks that slowly melt away. This event, known as "break-up," marks the unofficial start of spring in the Arctic.

As winter fades into spring, light and heat flood the tundra. The snow melts. Plants start growing again. The permafrost remains frozen, but the active layer of soil thaws. New roots spread through the ground, and decomposers resume their slow work.

During summer on the North Slope, daylight lasts more than eighteen hours every day. In Barrow, the Sun doesn't set at all from May 10 to August 2. It dips toward the horizon, but never drops below it. With this constant exposure to light, the tundra becomes a place of nonstop activity.

SUMMER ON THE NORTH SLOPE IS A TIME OF GROWTH. MANY FLOWERING PLANTS THRIVE DURING THE LONG HOURS OF SUNLIGHT.

Plants grow vigorously. Flowers bloom exuberantly. Bees, flies, and mosquitoes buzz endlessly. Waterfowl shuttle between their nests and their feeding grounds. Raptors soar overhead, while foxes and weasels slip through the meadows in search of prey.

As long as there is sunlight, plants can keep photosynthesizing. This means that, during the summer, tundra plants have more growing hours than plants that live hundreds of miles to the south. Still, the growing season lasts only about seventy days, and temperatures remain cool. In Barrow, the daytime temperature in July averages just 39° Fahrenheit (4° Celsius). Frost can occur at any time.

In autumn, the days shorten as quickly as they lengthened in spring. The temperature drops below freezing every night. Plants grow more slowly and store carbohydrates in their roots. They develop buds that will survive the winter and burst out with new growth the following spring. Some animals store food underground, while others increase their fat reserves. Insects and decomposers become dormant, or inactive. Caribou, wolves, and most birds head south. As the tundra grows colder, "freeze-up" occurs. Once again, ice cloaks the rivers, lakes, and ocean.

For the next eight to nine months, it is winter on the tundra. Frigid winds sweep over the gently rolling land and temperatures plunge far below freezing. Despite the harsh conditions, almost all the birds and mammals that stay on the tundra remain active all winter. Foxes and weasels hunt living prey and scavenge meat from animals that have died. Voles and lemmings make tunnels and nests under the snow, where they can stay warm while they forage for stems or seeds. All through the long arctic winter, the ecosystem keeps working.

THREE ZONES OF LIFE

In all seasons, different communities of living things inhabit different areas of the North Slope ecosystem. The tundra thrives because it has many different habitats, or environments. Each habitat is home to different kinds of plants, which provide food for different kinds of animals.

There are three general zones in this ecosystem. Each one has its characteristic plant and animal residents, but the zones also overlap and blend with each other.

Most of the low hills in the southern half of the ecosystem are covered with vast meadows of cottongrass. Because the cottongrass forms big clumps of vegetation called tussocks, this area is referred to as tussock tundra. The ground between tussocks is moist, but not wet. There are few ponds in this part of the ecosystem. Collared lemmings and red foxes live here year-round, and birds such as the American golden plover and the northern wheatear nest here in summer.

Farther north, the land is flatter and lower. Marshes, ponds, and lakes cover much of the landscape. Mosses blanket the ground, even growing under the water in shallow ponds. Grasslike plants called water sedges poke up above the mosses. This area's two dominant plant types give it its name—sedge-moss tundra. Brown lemmings and snowy owls make their homes here. Millions of geese, ducks, and wading birds nest here every summer.

A third distinct community of organisms lives along the rivers that flow through both the tussock tundra and the sedge-moss tundra. This is the riparian zone. Because the moving water wears away the land and exposes areas of permafrost to heat from the Sun, the active layer of soil is deeper here than anywhere else on the tundra. Willow and alder shrubs—the tallest plants on the tundra—crowd the riverbanks. Arctic foxes and arctic ground squirrels dig dens in the soft soil. Songbirds nest in the tall shrubs, and raptors nest on bluffs high above the river.

While some animals stay within one zone of the ecosystem their entire lives, others move back and forth between zones. Arctic foxes den in riverbanks, but range far out over the sedge-moss tundra in search of food. American golden plovers nest on the tussock tundra, but forage along shorelines in the sedge-moss tundra. Many species, such as caribou and Canada geese, come to the North Slope in summer to raise their young and feast on the lush tundra vegetation. In fall, they migrate south to places where food will be easier to find during the long winter.

(ABOVE) **ARCTIC WILLOW *(SALIX ARCTICA)* IS ONE OF THE FEW TUNDRA PLANTS THAT GROWS TO BE SEVERAL FEET HIGH.**

(TOP LEFT) **COTTONGRASS *(ERIOPHORUM)* COVERS A MEADOW NESTLED AT THE FOOT OF THE BROOKS RANGE.**

(BOTTOM LEFT) **WATER SEDGES *(CAREX AQUATILIS)* ARE AN IMPORTANT PART OF THE TUNDRA ECOSYSTEM.**

Even for year-round residents of the North Slope tundra, the borders between the three habitat zones are not sharp. Small differences in depth of the active layer, protection from the wind, or amount of water on the ground can make a big difference in which plants grow in a given spot. Patches of sedge-moss plants occur in damp, low-lying areas of tussock tundra. Similarly, patches of tussock plants spring up in elevated areas of sedge-moss tundra, where the soil is drier than on the surrounding plain. Rivers, and their riparian plant communities, cross both zones.

Because each plant community attracts different kinds of animals, the tundra may best be described as a mosaic of different habitats. Each plant and animal community thrives in the habitat that is best suited to it. Yet no part of the tundra is isolated from the rest. Each community interacts with and relies upon the others. Together, they make up the thriving ecosystem we know as the arctic tundra of Alaska's North Slope.

CARIBOU (RANGIFER TARANDUS)

CHAPTER 2
TUSSOCK TUNDRA

Tussock tundra stretches for miles across the rolling hills just north of the Brooks Range. Most of the land here is drier than in other areas of the tundra, making it the perfect place for tussock-forming cottongrass to grow. The leaves and stems of one cottongrass plant form a tussock, a clump of vegetation about the size of a soccer ball. Each clump is attached to the ground by a narrow stalk. The plant's long, thin leaves and puffy white flowers reach up to 3 feet (0.9 meter) above that.

Cottongrass tussocks may be the dominant plants on the tussock tundra, but many mosses, wildflowers, and shrubs also thrive in this environment.

COTTONGRASS TUSSOCKS MAY BE THE DOMINANT PLANTS ON THE TUSSOCK TUNDRA, BUT MANY MOSSES, WILDFLOWERS, AND SHRUBS ALSO THRIVE IN THIS ENVIRONMENT.

The vegetation is lush. There's hardly a bare patch of soil anywhere. Mosses grow in the low, damp ground between tussocks. Rodents, insects, and worms burrow through the soft clumps of moss to hide from hungry predators.

Hills and ridges provide habitat for plants that grow well on drier ground. Water drains downhill from these sites. They are also more exposed to the winter wind, which dries the ground by blowing away much of the snow that might supply meltwater in spring. In warm weather, the colorful blossoms of saxifrages, louseworts, and other forbs brighten the dry slopes of the tussock tundra. Forbs are nonwoody plants that are often called wildflowers.

Dwarf heath shrubs such as arctic blueberry and lingonberry also grow on dry sites. Most are less than 12 inches (30 centimeters) tall and have woody stems and wintergreen leaves. Unlike the deciduous shrubs that grow in most areas of the United States, wintergreen plants don't lose their leaves in autumn. Their leaves stay attached all winter long, so the plants can start photosynthesizing as soon as the snow disappears in spring. When new leaves grow in a few weeks later, the older leaves finally fall off. Dwarf heath shrubs grow slowly, and their wintergreen leaves give them a head start—a big advantage in a place with such a short growing season.

Many tundra plants come in different sizes and shapes depending on where they grow. The drier and windier the spot, the shorter the plant. In sheltered spots, dwarf willows may be several feet high. But in

(ABOVE) **ARCTIC BLUEBERRY (VACCINIUM ULIGINOSUM)**

(LEFT) **DURING THE SHORT SUMMER, FORBS, OR WILDFLOWERS, DOT THE TUSSOCK TUNDRA WITH THEIR VIBRANT COLORS.**

places where they are exposed to the wind, they grow outward rather than upward. On dry, windy hilltops, one-hundred-year-old willows might sprawl across 10 feet (3 meters) of ground, but be less than 1 foot (30 centimeters) tall, with "trunks" less than 1 inch (3 centimeters) thick.

Cushion plants and lichens grow in the driest, windiest areas of the tussock tundra. Cushion plants are forbs that form small lumps, or "cushions," of vegetation. One of the most common is the arctic dryad. In summer, its creamy white flowers float on slender stems that rise above the ground-hugging leaves.

Lichens are among the toughest organisms on Earth. They can survive long periods of dryness, darkness, and intense cold. While some look like splashes of paint on a rock, others resemble crusty mushrooms attached to the ground by a narrow stalk. Still others look like undersea corals or miniature tree branches. Few animals eat lichens because they taste awful.

Many people think a lichen is a plant, but it is actually a partnership between a fungus and an alga. The fungus forms the main structure of the lichen, absorbs water, and makes the bad-tasting chemicals that protect it from being eaten by herbivores. The algal cells inside the lichen carry out photosynthesis. The carbohydrates they make nourish both the alga and its fungal partner.

A HAVEN FOR HERBIVORES

Herbivores of all sizes live on the tussock tundra, from insects to mouselike rodents to large herd animals. The animals gain nourishment from eating plants, but the plants gain something too. The soil they grow in is fertilized by animal droppings. Animals spread plant seeds to new areas. Some plants, such as sedges, grow better if they are grazed than if they are left alone.

Many tundra plants rely on flies and bumblebees to pollinate them, or bring pollen to the central parts of their flowers so seeds can form. The powdery pollen contains sperm, or male sex cells. The center of a flower contains the plant's eggs, or female sex cells. When a flower is pollinated, sperm are able to unite with eggs to produce seeds. Some plants make seeds that are covered by a hard coat or shell. Other plants surround their seeds with a tasty fruit, such as a berry.

On the tundra, huge bumblebees pollinate flowers as they gather nectar, a sweet, energy-rich liquid found inside flowers. The bees also eat pollen, which is a good source of protein. They need these nutritious foods to produce young. As a bumblebee feeds, pollen sticks to bristly hairs on its body and legs. When the bee lands on another flower, a few grains of pollen fall onto the central parts of that blossom, and pollination occurs.

On cool mornings, bumblebees warm up for their foraging flights by sitting inside a flower for an hour or longer. Many tundra flowers have a broad, open shape, like a satellite dish. The petals gather light from the Sun and focus it on the center of the flower. This warms up the parts of the flower where the seeds will develop—and makes a convenient place for bees to sunbathe. After soaking up the warmth inside these bright blossoms, bumblebees take to the air again.

Lemmings and voles are just as important in the tundra ecosystem as bumblebees. These small rodents eat more plant material than any other species on the North Slope tundra. They are the main source of food for predators such as foxes and raptors. A lemming resembles a hamster. It has a plump body, a stubby tail, short ears, and a blunt snout. A vole looks more like a mouse. It has a slimmer body, a longer tail, and a more pointed snout than a lemming.

Both lemmings and voles make runways across the ground as they trample

SOUTHERN RED-BACKED VOLE (CLETHRIONOMYS GAPPERI)

the plants along their favorite routes. They also tunnel through the thick vegetation.

Two other important herbivores that roam the tussock tundra are caribou and musk oxen. Caribou are deerlike animals that grow and shed their antlers every year. They are the only species in the deer family in which both males and females grow antlers. Alaskan caribou belong to the same species as the reindeer that live in northern Europe.

Each year, four large herds of caribou come to the North Slope in early summer. Each herd has its own calving area, where the females give birth to their young. Some calving grounds are on tussock tundra, while others are farther north, near the coast. Caribou graze on many kinds of plants, including willows, true grasses, forbs, and cottongrass. When winter approaches, most of the caribou migrate to areas south of the Brooks Range. But a few thousand caribou stay on the North Slope all year. In winter, they find food by scraping through the snow with their large hooves to reach buried vegetation.

The biggest herbivores on the tundra are musk oxen. With their hulking forms,

(ABOVE) **CARIBOU *(RANGIFER TARANDUS)* GRAZE ON SEDGES AND OTHER PLANTS OF THE NORTH SLOPE.**

(LEFT) **A LEMMING RUNWAY**

massive horns, and long coats that nearly brush the ground, musk oxen look like prehistoric creatures. An adult male stands about 5 feet (nearly 2 meters) high at the shoulder and weighs between 600 and 800 pounds (270–360 kilograms). Females are about 1 foot (0.3 meter) shorter and 200 to 300 pounds (90 to 140 kilograms) lighter.

In autumn, every musk ox grows an undercoat of dense wool called qiviut. All winter long, qiviut keeps the musk ox warm, while its shaggy outer coat repels water and snow. In spring, when musk oxen shed their undercoats, clouds of grayish-brown qiviut dot the landscape. Birds and rodents use the soft wool to line their nests.

Musk oxen eat many kinds of tundra plants, including willows and other dwarf shrubs. They have trouble walking on and scraping through the snow, so in winter they forage on hills where the wind has blown away most of the snow.

A SUMMER HOME FOR BIRDS

Many species of birds come to the North Slope's tussock tundra in summer to find mates, make nests, and raise young. Some eat leaves, seeds, or berries. Others feed on insects or catch larger prey, such as lemmings.

Among the area's summer residents are many songbirds and shorebirds. Songbirds are small perching birds like those you might see at a backyard bird feeder. The rich tussock meadows offer them plenty of insects and seeds to eat. For birds that nest on the ground, such as Lapland longspurs, or those that nest in rock crevices, such as snow buntings and northern wheatears, the tussock tundra makes a fine home.

Most tundra songbirds change their diet depending on what's available. Northern wheatears are a good example. In early summer, when they are raising their young and need extra protein, wheatears eat bumblebees. They are the only bird species on the North Slope that relies on bumblebees as a main source of food. In late summer, after their chicks have left the nest and most of the bumblebees have died, they eat seeds and berries.

(ABOVE) **NORTHERN WHEATEAR**
(OENANTHE OENANTHE)

(LEFT) **MUSK OX** *(OVIBOS MOSCHATUS)*

(BELOW) **LAPLAND LONGSPUR**
(CALCARIUS LAPPONICUS)

(TOP) **AMERICAN GOLDEN PLOVER**
(PLUVIALIS DOMINICA)

(BOTTOM) **GOLDEN PLOVER EGGS ARE DIFFICULT FOR EVEN THE MOST SHARP-EYED PREDATOR TO SEE. THEIR BROWN SPOTS CAMOUFLAGE THEM PERFECTLY ON THE MOTTLED TUNDRA FLOOR.**

Several kinds of shorebirds nest on the tussock tundra, including plovers, whimbrels, and bar-tailed godwits. Although these birds forage along the shores of ponds and the ocean, they prefer to nest on dry ground. Since dry ground is rare near the coast, many adult shorebirds become commuters. Every day they fly north to the coastal wetlands in search of food, while their chicks remain high and dry on the rolling hills of the tussock tundra.

One of these commuter species is the American golden plover. These birds make their nests in shallow depressions on the ground. Their eggs are flecked with dark spots that make them almost impossible to see. If a fox or other predator approaches a nest, one of the parents tries to distract the hunter by pretending to be hurt. The bird drags a wing, limps, and cries out as if in pain. After it leads the predator far enough from the nest, the adult plover flies to safety. Later, when the predator has left the area, the bird returns to its nest.

In autumn, all the songbirds and shorebirds leave the North Slope. They wouldn't be able to find food on the tundra in winter. The shorebirds migrate to places much farther south, where temperatures are warm and food is abundant. Some of the songbirds also go far south, but many migrate just a short distance to central Alaska. There, temperatures may be even colder than on the North Slope, but seeds and berries are plentiful.

Songbirds and shorebirds are important members of the ecosystem. Their eggs and chicks are vital sources of food for predators, and their droppings fertilize the nutrient-poor soil so plants can grow better. In return, the North Slope tundra gives them a good place to raise their young. Even though these birds live on the tundra only during the summer, the energy the birds gain during their summers contributes to the ecosystems where they spend the rest of the year.

A PLACE FOR PREDATORS

With its millions of lemmings and voles, and thousands of bird families in summer, the North Slope's tussock tundra makes a rich hunting ground for predators. Some birds are predators, catching and eating insects, rodents, or the chicks of other birds. The tussock tundra is also home to mammalian predators such as foxes, weasels, wolves, and bears.

Two kinds of foxes live on the North Slope. Red foxes are common close to the mountains, and arctic foxes are common closer to the coast. Wherever the two species overlap, such as on tussock tundra, red foxes dominate.

Red foxes are 22 to 32 inches (56 to 81 centimeters) long with orange red fur, black "socks," and a white-tipped tail. Arctic foxes are smaller and have shorter snouts. Their fur is grayish brown during the summer and pure white in winter. Both kinds of foxes eat rodents, small birds, eggs, berries, and scavenged meat.

While foxes range far across the tundra as they hunt, weasels prowl the small spaces in thick vegetation. These fierce carnivores are closely related to ferrets and otters. They have long, thin bodies that are no bigger around than their heads. Any hole a weasel's head can fit into, its whole body can pass through. They easily slip through gaps in the vegetation as they hunt for rodents.

Weasels hunt at any time of day or night, and find their prey mainly by scent. They must be skilled hunters because they need to eat almost half their weight in food every day. Nursing females eat even more. During the weeks she is raising her young, a mother weasel eats about four lemmings or voles every day.

Two species of weasels live on the tundra. Short-tailed weasels grow up to 15 inches (38 centimeters) long and weigh 7 ounces (200 grams). Least weasels are about half that size, but just as fierce. In summer, both species have brown backs and pale bellies. In winter, both turn white with a bit of black at the tips of their tails.

Foxes and weasels stay on the North Slope all year, but two other carnivores, wolves and grizzly bears, usually retreat south when winter comes. Wolves range over wide areas, following the caribou on their yearly migrations. They also follow groups of musk oxen. Wolves usually can't kill a healthy adult musk ox. But a pack of wolves working together can separate a calf from its protective elders and kill it. Wolves also catch and eat smaller prey, such as lemmings and nesting birds. They return to the mountains in autumn, along with the caribou.

Unlike wolves, which hunt and travel in packs, grizzly bears live and hunt alone. Grizzlies are common in the Brooks Range and in other parts of Alaska. Fewer live on the North Slope. They come down from the mountains in summer to feast on berries, rodents, caribou, and musk oxen. In autumn, they return to their mountain homes, where they sleep through the winter in underground dens.

From grizzly bears to bumblebees, and from cottongrass to lichens, the rolling hills of the tussock tundra are home to dozens of species of plants, herbivores, and carnivores. As full of life as it is, it seems quiet compared to the sedge-moss tundra to its north.

CHAPTER 3
SEDGE-MOSS TUNDRA

As the rolling terrain of the Brooks Range foothills gives way to the lower, flatter land near the coast, the vegetation gradually changes. Cottongrass tussocks disappear, and the ground becomes soggy. The low coastal plain is dotted with ponds and marshes. This is the sedge-moss tundra. It is one of the largest, richest wetlands in North America.

Even though the sedge-moss tundra occupies a low plain, it is not completely flat. Its small mounds and ridges are only a few feet high, but that is high enough to create habitats with different amounts of water in the soil and different types of wind exposure. The result is a patchwork of different plant and animal communities.

EVEN THOUGH IT RECEIVES LESS PRECIPITATION THAN MANY DESERTS, THE SEDGE-MOSS TUNDRA IS ONE OF THE BIGGEST WETLANDS IN NORTH AMERICA. THE GROUND REMAINS SOGGY ALL SUMMER BECAUSE WATER FROM RAIN AND SNOWMELT CAN'T DRAIN DOWN THROUGH THE PERMAFROST.

PRIMARY PRODUCERS: SEDGES

Sedges are among the most important plants on the tundra. Two habitat zones—tussock tundra and sedge-moss tundra—are named for this group of plants. Sedges carry on much of the photosynthesis that occurs in the ecosystem, converting solar energy into carbohydrates. In turn, sedges are an essential source of food for herbivores such as lemmings, geese, and caribou. Sedges are closely related to grasses. They look much like grasses, but their leaf blades are often three sided rather than flat.

Some sedges have fluffy white flowers that give rise to their common name, "cottongrass." Four species of cottongrass grow on Alaska's North Slope, but only one, *Eriophorum vaginatum*, forms tussocks. This species provides shelter as well as food for tundra animals. As a tussock soaks up heat from the Sun, the air around the plant warms up several degrees. This helps neighboring plants grow faster, and attracts insects and rodents.

Other species of sedges grow in and around ponds on the sedge-moss tundra. They provide shelter and food for aquatic insects and nesting birds. The most common species is the water sedge, *Carex aquatilis.*

Most of the sedge leaves that die each year don't decay. Instead, they fall to the ground and accumulate as peat. A few of the dead sedge leaves continue to be used by tundra animals. Birds, lemmings, and voles use some of the dead leaves to line their nests. Decomposers break down others and return nutrients to the soil.

THE LAY OF THE LAND

If you had a chance to fly over the North Slope's sedge-moss tundra, you would see large expanses of patterned ground—land with dozens of large crisscrossing cracks. These cracks resemble the ones that form in mud after a puddle dries up, but on a much bigger scale. On the arctic tundra, the cracks have formed slowly over time as a result of the area's cycle of freezing and thawing.

As winter begins, temperatures drop below freezing at night, but warm up again during the day. The same thing happens in spring, as the land slowly warms up.

During these swings in temperature, the active layer of soil freezes and thaws repeatedly. Each night, water in the soil freezes and expands. This places tremendous stress on the soil, causing it to crack on the surface. When it warms up the next day, water from the surface drains into the cracks. In spring, melting snow adds even more water. When the temperature drops again, the pooled water freezes and forms a wedge of ice in each crack. Every wedge pokes down into the permafrost and presses against the sides of the crack, forcing nearby soil to bulge upward. Only the top of the ice wedge melts every summer. The rest of the wedge, surrounded by permafrost deep in the ground, stays frozen.

Each winter, the ice wedge grows a little wider, pierces a little deeper into the ground, and displaces even more nearby soil. Small ridges of soil begin to rise on either side of the crack. As years pass, the ridges grow higher and higher.

> IF YOU HAD A CHANCE TO FLY OVER THE NORTH SLOPE'S SEDGE-MOSS TUNDRA, YOU WOULD SEE LARGE EXPANSES OF PATTERNED GROUND—LAND WITH DOZENS OF LARGE CRISSCROSSING CRACKS.

Most ice wedges on the Alaskan tundra are a few feet wide at the top, but some are much larger. Scientists have found one ice wedge that measures 33 feet (10 meters) across. It is about fourteen thousand years old.

As the wedges grow longer, they meet and cross other wedges to create polygon patterns. A polygon is a shape with many sides. Most tundra polygons have four, five, or six sides. Small tundra polygons are about 30 feet (9 meters) wide, while large ones may be more than 200 feet (60 meters) across. Polygons cover vast areas of the sedge-moss tundra, so that from the air, the land looks like a giant honeycomb.

HABITATS BY HEIGHT

The most common arrangement of patterned ground is made up of low-center polygons. The ridges of soil that surround each polygon are higher than the land in the center of the polygon. The ridges remain fairly dry, while rain and meltwater drain down into the low center of the polygon.

Many polygons collect so much water in their centers that marshes, ponds, and

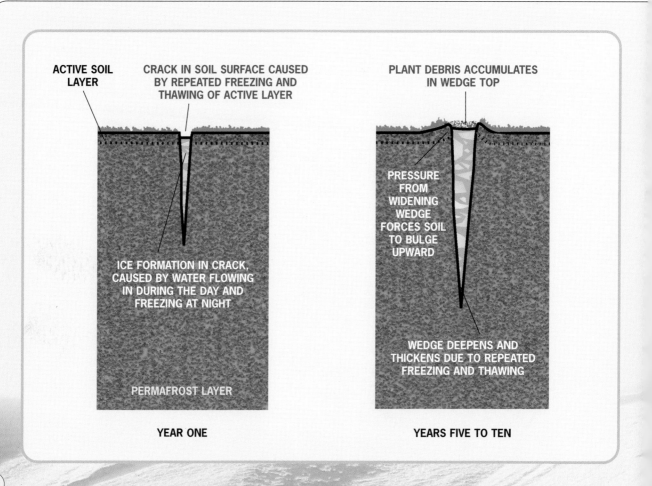

ACTIVE SOIL LAYER

CRACK IN SOIL SURFACE CAUSED BY REPEATED FREEZING AND THAWING OF ACTIVE LAYER

ICE FORMATION IN CRACK, CAUSED BY WATER FLOWING IN DURING THE DAY AND FREEZING AT NIGHT

PERMAFROST LAYER

YEAR ONE

PLANT DEBRIS ACCUMULATES IN WEDGE TOP

PRESSURE FROM WIDENING WEDGE FORCES SOIL TO BULGE UPWARD

WEDGE DEEPENS AND THICKENS DUE TO REPEATED FREEZING AND THAWING

YEARS FIVE TO TEN

lakes form. Water completely covers the active layer of soil. Fungi and other decomposers can't live in such a wet environment. As a result, when the plants growing in these areas die, they barely decompose at all. Instead, they sink to the bottom and become peat.

Over time, the peat builds up so much that the center of the polygon—the area that had been underwater—begins to rise. Eventually, the pile of peat grows higher than the ridges of soil around the edge of the polygon. The polygon pattern remains, but now the center is higher and drier

than the borders. Scientists call this a high-center polygon.

Sometimes a low-center polygon meets a different fate. The border around it breaks open, and the water drains out of the pond in the center. Now the muddy bottom is exposed to the air. When it freezes, water in the mud forms a solid lump of ice below ground. Over years of freezing and thawing, the lump grows, pushing the soil around it outward and upward. Each year, the soil bulges higher. Gradually, a cone-shaped hill rises above the surrounding land. Now it is called

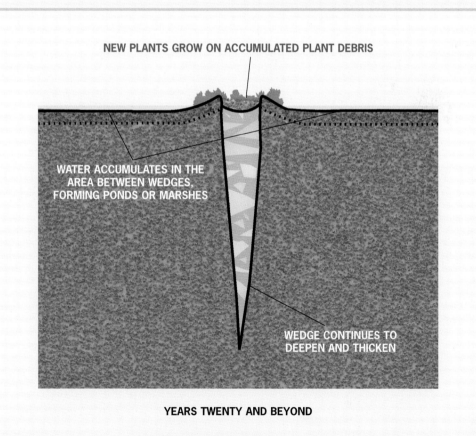

NEW PLANTS GROW ON ACCUMULATED PLANT DEBRIS

WATER ACCUMULATES IN THE AREA BETWEEN WEDGES, FORMING PONDS OR MARSHES

WEDGE CONTINUES TO DEEPEN AND THICKEN

YEARS TWENTY AND BEYOND

a pingo. The largest pingos are about 250 feet (75 meters) high. Whatever its size, a pingo's core is made of solid ice.

LIFE ON THE LAND

The mosaic of wet and dry habitats on the sedge-moss tundra makes it possible for different plant communities to live very close to one another. The ponds and marshes are home to sedges, mosses, and grasses. The sedges in these ponds do not form tussocks. Instead, they grow as single blades scattered throughout the pond. Mosses are primitive plants that form low mounds of soft vegetation. The brilliant greens and deep reds of different moss species provide some of the sedge-moss tundra's brightest colors. Like other plants, mosses convert solar energy to carbohydrates. Unlike most other plants, they do not pass on much of that energy to herbivores. Few animals will eat mosses, even if they are very hungry.

Plants that need a drier environment, such as dwarf heath shrubs, forbs, and lichens, thrive on ridges, peat mounds, and pingos. The slopes of a pingo, especially those facing south, receive more sunlight than the surrounding land. They also have drier soil because water is able to drain downhill. The extra heat and better drainage create a deep active layer that supports shrubs and forbs that cannot live in flatter parts of the sedge-moss tundra.

Each of these plant communities provides food and living space for different kinds of animals. For example, two species of lemmings live on the sedge-moss tundra. Brown lemmings and collared lemmings both have brown fur in summer. Collared lemmings also have a ring of darker fur around their shoulders. Brown lemmings stay brown in winter, but collared lemmings grow a coat of white fur. They are the only rodents in the world that turn white in winter.

Collared lemmings prefer plants that grow on dry ground, such as willows, dryads, and saxifrages. They are common on the tussock tundra as well as on drier areas of the sedge-moss tundra. Brown lemmings are more at home on marshy ground, where they eat the lush stems of water plants.

THE LEMMING POPULATION CYCLE

Lemmings are the most important herbivores in the North Slope tundra ecosystem. They eat huge amounts of vegetation and are eaten by almost every kind of predator.

Lemming populations go through cycles every three to six years. When food is plentiful and the weather is good, lemmings reproduce so quickly that their population explodes. Hundreds of thousands of lemmings swarm over the tundra. Arctic foxes, weasels, snowy owls, and other predators feast on the abundant prey. With plenty of food for themselves and their young, predator populations rise.

As more and more lemmings crowd the tundra, they devour more sedges and willows. They even dig into the soil and gobble up the plants' roots. Eventually, the plants can't grow fast enough to replace what the lemmings eat. As plants struggle to survive, lemmings start running out of food.

The crowded, hungry rodents fight among themselves. Sometimes they kill and eat each other. They swarm over the tundra, searching for a place that is less crowded, but they rarely find one. Thousands of lemmings starve, get sick, or fall prey to predators. Then the lemming population crashes.

COLLARED LEMMING
(DICROSTONYX TORQUATUS)

With the lemming population low, predators struggle to survive. Some leave the tundra in search of food. Others stay, but do not breed because they would not be able to feed their young. Many predators starve.

Although a low lemming population hurts predators, it gives plants a chance to grow back and provide food for the few lemmings that remain. Within a year or two, the lemmings are thriving again, and all the organisms that depend on them thrive again too.

Lemmings are not the only tundra animals that go through population cycles. But lemmings are so important as consumers of plants and as food for carnivores that their ups and downs have a much greater impact on the ecosystem than population swings among other species.

ARCTIC FOXES *(ALOPEX LAGOPUS)* DIG IN THE SNOW, SEEKING LEMMINGS THAT HAVE BURROWED BELOW.

The two species of lemmings share runways as they scurry from place to place, each in search of its favorite food. They also swim well, a handy skill for animals living in an area with so much water. If a lemming smells food on the other side of a pond, it just jumps into the water and swims to its meal. Lemmings can cross lakes more than 0.5 mile (0.8 kilometer) wide.

Both species of lemmings stay active all winter long. When snow gently covers the plants surrounding their runways, the runways become tunnels. Snug in their maze of snow tunnels, lemmings continue to live much as they do in summer. They may even mate and raise young.

While they are under the snow, lemmings are safe from predators that hunt mainly by sight. But arctic foxes and weasels still pose a threat. Arctic foxes listen for the little scraping sounds of lemmings scampering through a tunnel. When they detect a lemming, they pounce and trap the rodent under their paws. Then they push the snow aside with their snout and grab the prey.

Because weasels have long, slender bodies, they are able to zip through the tunnels in pursuit of their prey.

For lemmings, spring is the most dangerous season on the sedge-moss tundra. As the snow melts, their tunnels flood. Some lemmings drown. Others freeze to death after getting wet. Without snow cover, lemmings also become more visible to predators such as snowy owls.

Adult snowy owls stand about 24 inches (61 centimeters) tall and have white feathers all year round. Snowy owls need a steady supply of lemmings to eat. When lemmings are abundant, snowies stay on the tundra in winter. But when lemmings are scarce, these birds may not mate or raise a family. They may even leave the tundra and fly south in search of food.

Like other owls, snowies regurgitate pellets of material they cannot digest, such as hair, bones, and teeth. Owl pellets are a source of nutrients for decomposers and even for other kinds of birds. Sandpipers pick them apart to find bones and teeth, which contain calcium the sandpipers need to make strong eggshells.

While snowy owls do most of their hunting at night, raptors, such as peregrine falcons and golden eagles, hunt during the day. Because pingos are much higher than the surrounding land, they give raptors a good place to perch as they scan the coastal tundra for prey. Most birds see well, but predatory birds have the sharpest vision of all. A raptor soaring high in the air or perched atop a pingo can spot a lemming running across a patch of moss more than 1,000 feet (400 meters) away. When the raptor spots a potential meal, it swoops down and grabs the prey in its talons. Then the swift hunter carries the prey away for its own meal, or to feed its growing chicks.

THRIVING WETLANDS

Pingos are important to the tundra ecosystem, but the most crucial habitat in the sedge-moss tundra is the wetlands. The area's scattered ponds and marshes are home to millions of insects, aquatic invertebrates, fish, and migratory birds.

The sedge-moss wetlands are ideal habitat for mollusks and crustaceans. Mollusks are shelled animals, such as clams and snails. Crustaceans are crayfish-like animals. The mollusks and crustaceans that live in tundra ponds are less than 1 inch (3 centimeters) long. Some are almost microscopic.

Some mollusks and crustaceans cling to plants. Others drift or swim through the water. Many live in the mud at the bottom of a pond. They eat a variety of foods, such as sedges, animal droppings, and dead plant matter. They also eat immature insects.

Mosquitoes, crane flies, midges, and black flies are some of the insects that start life as aquatic larvae. The adults, which can fly, lay their eggs in the water. After the larvae hatch, they feed and grow in the water before developing wings and becoming airborne adults. Millions of aquatic insect larvae cloud the tundra ponds in early and mid-summer. Later, adult insects fill the air. They swarm around mammals and birds, seeking warmth or a blood meal. Caribou sometimes wade into the ocean to escape them.

To caribou, the hordes of insects are a terrible nuisance, but the biting pests play an important role in the ecosystem. They are a major source of food for many of the

(ABOVE) **MIDGE (CHIRONOMIDAE)**

(LEFT) **CRANEFLY (TIPULIDAE)**

birds that come to the sedge-moss tundra every summer. The insects provide a much-needed source of protein while the birds are nesting and raising their young.

One of the busiest places on the North Slope is Teshekpuk Lake and the area around it. Each year, the 28,000 members of the Teshekpuk caribou herd come to the area to give birth to their calves and graze on lush sedges. In the process, they produce tons of droppings that fertilize the soil.

While caribou munch on plants and nurse their young, Teshekpuk Lake's fish feast on aquatic insects, mollusks, crustaceans, fish eggs, and smaller fish. Eleven species of fish live in the lake, including arctic cisco, ninespine stickleback, and several kinds of whitefish. Many of the lake's small fish fall prey to larger fish or the loons that nest nearby.

Every summer, millions of shorebirds and waterfowl nest along the lake's inlets, islands, and marshes. These birds nest on the ground, which makes them attractive prey for arctic foxes, weasels, and raptors. Some nest in large groups called colonies. Being in a large group helps the birds guard against predators because there are

PACIFIC LOONS *(GAVIA PACIFICA)* BUILD SOLITARY NESTS ALONG THE EDGES OF
TUNDRA LAKES AND PONDS.

more eyes watching for danger. Other bird species nest in more private spots, hidden by long sedges or on small islands where predators can't easily get to them.

Shorebirds such as sandpipers and plovers have long, thin legs like stilts. Most do not swim well. They hunt as they walk along the coastline or the edge of a pond. With their long bills, they pick up insects or probe into the mud to nab clams and other invertebrates that live below the surface.

All waterfowl are good swimmers. This group includes ducks, geese, swans, and loons. They eat fish, aquatic invertebrates, or aquatic plants. Most waterfowl spend the winter far south of the tundra, in places like California or Texas, but eiders are exceptions. These sea ducks live in the Arctic year round.

Three species of eiders breed on the North Slope—king eiders, spectacled eiders, and Steller's eiders. These birds range from 18 to 23 inches (46 to 58 centimeters) long and weigh 2 to 3 pounds (0.9 to 1.4 kilograms). During the summer, eiders build their nests on the sedge-moss tundra and forage for mollusks and crustaceans in nearby lakes. In winter they live on the Arctic Ocean, where gaps in the ice let them reach open water. During the coldest months of the year, eiders find food by diving deep into the icy sea.

WHERE LAND MEETS SEA

All across its northern border, the sedge-moss tundra meets the Arctic Ocean. The ocean makes this part of the North Slope cloudier and cooler than the tussock tundra farther inland. The ocean also provides food for eiders and many other tundra animals.

Jaegers (pronounced YAY-gurz) are large, dark gray gulls with hooked beaks. Their name is German for "hunter." Although jaegers sometimes hunt lemmings and small birds, they specialize in stealing food from other birds, such as terns. When a tern emerges from the chilly waters of the Arctic Ocean with a fish in its bill, a jaeger will rush in and try to steal the catch. Then the tern has to go hunting again.

EVEN THE BONES OF DEAD ANIMALS, LIKE THESE WHALE BONES, PLAY AN IMPORTANT ROLE IN THE TUNDRA ECOSYSTEM.

The ocean provides food for scavengers as well as for hunters. Seals and whales cruise near the shore as they hunt for fish and crustaceans. When one of these large marine mammals dies, its body may wash up on shore and provide a feast for gulls, ravens, foxes, and other scavengers. One bowhead whale, for example, weighs up to 60 tons (50 metric tons). Arctic foxes may stay near a dead whale for months, eating the meat and even sleeping inside the carcass as if it were a cave. A variety of insects benefit from the huge carcass too. Adults lay their eggs on the body. When the larvae hatch, they have plenty of food.

Eventually, only the dead animal's bones remain. But even those are used by tundra creatures. Birds perch on the bones for a better view of the surrounding landscape, lemmings and voles nest under them, and arctic foxes hide behind them as they stalk the rodents. Droppings from all these animals fertilize the ground around the skeleton. Over time, flowering plants sprout in the nutrient-rich soil. Decomposition happens so slowly on the tundra that the skeleton and its little oasis of flowers may decorate the coastline for more than one hundred years.

The sturdy bones provide a boost in height that brings new opportunities for many forms of life. The same thing happens, on a much larger scale, along the North Slope's rivers.

CHAPTER 4
ALONG THE RIVERS

Dozens of rivers cross the North Slope tundra. They carry rainfall and snowmelt from the mountains of the Brooks Range northward to the Arctic Ocean, passing through tussock tundra and sedge-moss tundra along the way. The land alongside each river is called the riparian zone.

As rivers flow across the North Slope, they erode, or wear away, the soil along their banks. In some places, the tundra is just a bit higher than a river flowing through it. But in areas where the water has cut through the soil more quickly, bluffs up to 150 feet (46 meters) high line the river.

All along these riverbanks, permafrost is exposed to the summer sun and warm air. As a result, the active layer of soil is up to 40 inches (100 centimeters) deep along riverbanks. In other tundra zones, it is only 8 to 20 inches (20 to 50 centimeters) deep. The deeper active layer makes the riparian zone a good home for plants and animals that don't live elsewhere on the tundra, such as tall shrubs and burrowing animals.

THE DEEPER ACTIVE LAYER MAKES THE RIPARIAN ZONE A GOOD HOME FOR PLANTS AND ANIMALS THAT DON'T LIVE ELSEWHERE ON THE TUNDRA, SUCH AS TALL SHRUBS AND BURROWING ANIMALS.

RICH SOIL, TALL PLANTS

Because rainwater and snowmelt drain into the rivers, the riparian soils are among the driest on the tundra. Drier soils hold more oxygen than wet soils, so decomposing organisms such as fungi and bacteria thrive in the deep, warm, oxygen-rich active layer. As a result, the soil along riverbanks contains more nutrients than other tundra soils. In turn, the richer soil supports a vigorous plant community.

The most abundant plants along riverbanks are willows and alders. In other areas of the North Slope tundra, these shrubs rarely grow taller than 2 feet (0.6 meter), but in the riparian zone they may grow more than 6 feet (2 meters) tall. They can grow taller along rivers for several reasons. The active layer is deep enough for the shrubs to put down large roots, and the roots get more oxygen and nutrients. In addition, the high riverbanks protect shrubs from the wind.

Tundra winds are especially harmful in winter, when they carry sharp crystals of ice and snow. Any plant that sticks up above snow level is struck and damaged by the crystals. Buds and twigs exposed to the wind become damaged, so the plant is unable to grow any taller. As a result, most tundra plants are no taller than the average depth of the snow that covers them each year. The tallest plants grow very close to the river, where huge snowdrifts keep them safe all winter long. Farther from the river, both the drifts and the plants are shorter.

Nestled beneath the willows and alders are smaller shrubs, such as dwarf birch, arctic blueberry, crowberry, and Labrador tea. Many of these plants produce nutritious berries that birds, rodents, and grizzly bears eat. Few animals eat shrubs' leaves or stems, though, because many produce chemicals that make them taste bad. Some are even poisonous. These shrubs grow very slowly, and if animals nibbled them often, they would have trouble recovering.

A few forbs speckle the riverbank with bright flowers, but the sedges and mosses that are so important in other tundra zones are much less common. Scattered clumps of moss grow in shady spots beneath the shrubs, but they do not form a continuous carpet as they do in sedge-moss tundra.

A HOME BASE FOR ANIMALS

Each riparian community is like a long ribbon laid out across the tundra.

The dense stands of tall shrubs form a corridor that allows forest animals, such as moose, to live far from their usual homes farther south. These creatures usually stay near the river their whole lives. But many other animals use the riparian zone as a "home base" from which they venture out onto the open tundra in search of food.

One of these is the arctic fox. Even though arctic foxes range far out over the sedge-moss and tussock tundra, they den along rivers, in peat mounds, or on the slopes of pingos. These are the only places in the ecosystem where the active layer is deep enough for the foxes to dig an underground home.

Another resident of the riparian zone is the arctic ground squirrel, also known as the siksik. These rodents eat plant seeds, stems, flowers, and roots. Like arctic foxes, siksiks forage in many areas of the tundra, but make their homes in places where the active layer is deep. Siksiks dig long networks of tunnels in riverbanks or on the slopes of pingos. They aid decomposing organisms in two ways—their excavations let more oxygen into the soil, and their wastes supply nutrients.

In summer almost every predator on the tundra hunts siksiks. The lively rodents are especially important as a source of food in years when the lemming population is low. In winter siksiks do not contribute to the flow of energy in the ecosystem because they hibernate. The siksik is the only North Slope mammal that sleeps through the winter. All the other year-round residents stay active during that harsh season.

When siksiks snuggle into their burrows for their long winter's nap, a raptor called the gyrfalcon (pronounced JER-fal-kun) has to adjust its diet. Unlike the ecosystem's other raptors, gyrfalcons stay on the tundra all year round. In summer, siksiks are their favorite food. But in winter, with siksiks out of reach underground, gyrfalcons eat mostly ptarmigan (pronounced TAR-mih-gun). These plump relatives of grouse and quail are the only herbivorous birds that stay on the arctic tundra year round. Two species live on the North Slope, rock ptarmigan

SECONDARY CONSUMER: ARCTIC FOX *(Alopex lagopus)*

Arctic foxes are smart, efficient hunters. These housecat-sized mammals also scavenge meat from dead animals and eat berries. When food is plentiful, arctic foxes bury their leftovers in shallow holes in the ground. Months later, they dig up the food and eat it. Sometimes the foxes dig up their stored food and then bury it again in the same spot, as if they are checking to make sure it is still there.

Although arctic foxes live alone most of the year, they seek out the same partner each year at breeding time. The adults prepare a snug den that extends 6 to 10 feet (2 to 3 meters) underground. Sometimes the foxes dig their den themselves, but they may also expand an old burrow made by other animals. Most den openings face south, so they get more sunlight and warmth. A fox pair often uses the same den summer after summer.

Foxes mate in April, while winter still grips the tundra. Their babies, called kits, are born in June. Newborn kits cannot see or hear, and they have no teeth. They grow quickly, and within three weeks they emerge from the den and begin to explore. Although each litter starts with about ten kits, very few survive to adulthood. Some die because their parents cannot find enough food. Other kits catch diseases or are killed and eaten by their siblings. In late summer, the fox family splits up. Each fox goes off on its own.

During the winter, arctic foxes may roam more than 600 miles (1,000 kilometers) from home in search of food. When it is time to sleep, they find a sheltered nook or nestle into a snowbank to get out of the wind. When spring returns, each parent fox goes back to its den to meet its mate and raise another family. Last year's kits, now nearly one year old, must find a mate and a den site to start a family of their own.

and willow ptarmigan. Both are 13 to 16 inches (33 to 41 centimeters) long and weigh 10 to 24 ounces (30 to 68 grams). Rock ptarmigan prefer higher, drier ground than willow ptarmigan, but both species eat the buds and twigs of willows and birches. In summer they take advantage of the booming population of insects and eat caterpillars as well.

Both species of ptarmigan spend summers along riverbanks or in sheltered, shrubby areas, such as the slopes of pingos. In winter they venture away from those areas, looking for food. When it's time to sleep, they stay warm by burrowing into a snowbank. Dense feathers on their feet keep ptarmigan warm and serve as snowshoes, helping the birds walk over the dry snow.

Ptarmigan are hunted by jaegers, snowy owls, arctic foxes, wolves, and gyrfalcons. Their camouflaged coloring helps them avoid these predators. In summer their mottled gray-brown feathers

ROCK PTARMIGAN *(LAGOPUS MUTUS)*
IN SUMMER PLUMAGE

ROCK PTARMIGAN IN WINTER PLUMAGE

blend in with the dappled sun and shadows along the rivers, and their white winter plumage makes them hard to spot in their snowy environment.

Ptarmigan and gyrfalcons stay on the North Slope all year, but the tundra's riverside corridors also provide important breeding grounds for many migratory birds. Songbirds called redpolls nest in willows and alders, while American tree sparrows nest in lower shrubs or on the ground. Raptors and Canada geese nest on high bluffs above the rivers. The stretch of the Colville River that flows through the sedge-moss tundra is especially important for migratory birds. It provides more nesting sites for songbirds than any other area in the ecosystem, and it is one of the busiest and most important raptor nesting areas in North America.

LIFE IN THE RIVERS

Tundra riverbanks teem with life, but the chilly rivers themselves have far fewer fish and insect residents than are found in rivers in warmer parts of the world. Despite the hardships of this environment, more than twenty species of fish live in the Colville and other large rivers of the North Slope. Many, such as the whitefish and the arctic cisco, forage along the coast during the summer, but swim upstream for the winter.

North Slope rivers offer little space and almost no food to overwintering fish. Wherever the water is less than 7 feet (2 meters) deep it freezes solid, so the fish must find deeper pools where they can wait out the long winter in safety. Some deep spots form in areas where the land has eroded away more deeply. Others form in spots where tree branches and other debris pile up and partially block the river's flow. Quiet pools form behind these natural dams.

In summer aquatic insects and other small aquatic animals graze on leaf litter in the slow-flowing water. In winter insects, mollusks, and crustaceans burrow into the mud or nestle deep into cracks between chunks of gravel. Because these animals remain dormant during the cold season, the river's fish may not eat until spring, when they return to the ocean to feast on mollusks and tiny creatures called zooplankton.

RIVERS THROUGH TIME

Like rivers everywhere, tundra rivers change over time. As their courses shift, deep spots fill in and shallow spots deepen. In some places, sandbars and islands form. Each new area of land becomes home to a new community of plants and animals.

Usually, the first plants to colonize these sites are willows that were uprooted by a flood upstream. Most plants die if they are flooded and torn up, but not willows. When they land on a new spot, they quickly sprout new roots to anchor themselves. Over time, the river deposits more sand and soil around them. Seeds of forbs and grasses, carried by water, wind, or animals, sprout in the new soil. Green alders soon join the young community.

As the willows and alders grow, they shade the ground beneath them. Some of the forbs and grasses that first populated the sandbar cannot survive in a shady environment. Over several years, they are replaced by shade-loving mosses.

After several decades, the original willows begin to age. Younger willows crowd the sandbar. The ground beneath them is almost completely shaded. Mosses cover more of the soil, keeping it cool in summer. As a result, the soil doesn't thaw as deeply as it did in previous years, and the active layer shrinks. The roots of large plants have trouble holding on in the shallower soil. Eventually, the trees topple, and the ground is once again exposed to sunlight. As the active layer warms and deepens again, new willows sprout or take root, and the cycle of plant growth begins anew.

Even with all the changes they go through, the North Slope's riparian ribbons continue to provide habitat for a wide variety of plants and animals. They also link tussock and sedge-moss communities and help many species of animals use more than one habitat. This flexibility is crucial to the ecosystem's health and survival.

CHAPTER 5

MAINTAINING THE BALANCE

On tussock meadows in early summer, bumblebees visit flowers to eat their protein-rich pollen and drink their energy-rich nectar. Grains of pollen stick to the bumblebees and later get brushed off on the reproductive parts of other flowers, which are then able to make seeds or berries.

At around the same time, northern wheatears arrive from their winter homes in eastern Asia. They nest on high ground in the tussock meadows and feed on bumblebees. Using energy from the pollen and nectar the bumblebees ate, the northern wheatears lay eggs and feed their young. Over the next few weeks, some of the wheatear chicks fall prey to weasels, which then gain the energy and nutrients they need to help their own young grow strong.

When wheatears and weasels produce feces and urine, decomposers process these wastes. Nutrients that powered the bumblebees, northern wheatears, and weasels return to the soil to nourish the flowering plants once more.

In late summer, most of the bumblebees die. The northern wheatears begin to eat seeds and berries, many of which formed following pollination by the bumblebees several weeks earlier.

BUMBLEBEE (BOMBUS)

This example shows many of the links among the tundra ecosystem's plants and animals. As each species cares for itself, it also does work that helps other species. Pollination, reproduction, nourishing young, and the recycling of nutrients are jobs that require participation by many members of the ecosystem.

All of these jobs are done in every ecosystem, but on the North Slope tundra, there are fewer species to do them. A job done by eight or ten species in a temperate forest or on an African grassland might be done by a single species on the tundra. For example, there are more than twenty thousand species of bees in the world, but only two of them live on the North Slope. In other ecosystems, every species is important. On the arctic tundra, every species is *crucial.*

AS EACH SPECIES CARES FOR ITSELF, IT ALSO DOES WORK THAT HELPS OTHER SPECIES. POLLINATION, REPRODUCTION, NOURISHING YOUNG, AND THE RECYCLING OF NUTRIENTS ARE JOBS THAT REQUIRE PARTICIPATION BY MANY MEMBERS OF THE ECOSYSTEM.

This makes the North Slope tundra more vulnerable to disruptions than many other ecosystems on Earth. An ecosystem's ability to recover from damage depends on its biodiversity—how many different species it supports. The tundra's ability to bounce back is limited by its low biodiversity. Losing one of its two species of bees, for example, would spell disaster for North Slope plants and the animals that depend on them.

ANIMALS ON THE MOVE

Biodiversity is lower on the tundra than in most other ecosystems because few species can survive in a place where winter lasts for eight months every year. Biodiversity on the tundra would be even lower if it didn't have so many different habitats available so close to one another. Each habitat supports a different community of plants. Most animals move around, so they can take advantage of what each habitat has to offer.

Siksiks den along rivers or in peat mounds, but look for food all over the tundra. Semipalmated sandpipers nest on dry ridges that border polygons, but eat mollusks they find in marshy areas. Canada geese nest on bluffs above the Colville River, but travel to the sedge-moss tundra to eat water sedges growing in ponds. Even small animals, such as lemmings, can easily travel between patches of dry ground and marshy polygons.

Some animals roam even farther afield in winter, when food is harder to find. Ptarmigan venture away from the shelter of the riparian zone. Arctic foxes may not even stay on land. When the surface of the Arctic Ocean freezes over and becomes locked to the shore, arctic foxes travel across the ice as if it were land. They range far from shore, following polar bears as they hunt seals. A polar bear hunts by waiting near holes in the ice. When a seal pokes its head up to get a breath of air, the polar bear grabs it. After the polar bear finishes its meal, an arctic fox can dart in and clean up the leftovers.

Just as few tundra animals stay in one habitat their whole lives, few fill only one role in the ecosystem. Instead, they are opportunists, eating different kinds of foods depending on what's available. Few herbivores eat only seeds or only sedge stems. They don't even limit their diet entirely to plants.

In summer ptarmigan eat caterpillars as well as willow buds. Siksiks won't kill other animals, but they will eat meat if they find an animal that's already dead.

Similarly, few carnivores eat only fresh meat from animals they have killed. Almost all secondary consumers occasionally scavenge meat from carcasses. Some even eat plant material, such as berries and seeds. Gyrfalcons stick to an all-meat diet, but they eat different prey depending on the season—siksiks in summer, ptarmigan in winter. Arctic foxes may be the tundra's champion opportunists. They eat bird eggs and chicks in early summer, berries in late summer, seal scraps in winter, and lemmings whenever they can get them.

SUMMER ON THE TUNDRA

Biodiversity on the North Slope tundra increases dramatically in spring, when caribou, wolves, and dozens of species of birds arrive. These animals couldn't survive on the tundra in winter because they would not be able to find food. But in summer, the tundra offers an ideal home for them. It provides abundant food and plenty of open country in which to raise young.

Although migrants are on the tundra for only a few months each year, they are as necessary to the ecosystem as the animals that stay all year. Migratory animals also link the North Slope tundra to other ecosystems, some right next door and others halfway around the world. The migrants gain from and contribute to each place they live. In the process, they provide a channel through which energy and nutrients can flow from one ecosystem to another.

Animal migrations have been an important part of the North Slope tundra ecosystem for thousands of years. Long ago, land animals such as caribou, moose, and wolves were able to cross the Bering land bridge that linked Alaska and Siberia. Today, the Bering Sea covers the former land bridge, but the North Slope tundra still borders three other ecosystems: the Arctic Ocean on the north and west, the mountains of the Brooks Range to the south, and boreal forest to the southeast. Migratory animals connect the tundra to all three.

Large fish such as arctic cisco link the North Slope with the ocean. They feed in coastal waters in summer, but spend winters in deep tundra lakes or river pools. The seals and whales that sometimes wash up on shore never live on the tundra, but their remains are an important source of food for North Slope scavengers.

Grizzly bears and wolves retreat south for the winter. While grizzlies sleep through most of the winter in cavelike dens, wolves stay active, hunting lemmings, moose, caribou, and other prey.

When caribou return to the tundra in spring, they become especially important members of the tundra ecosystem. They graze sedges, grasses, and willows throughout the North Slope. They provide food for some of the smallest animals—biting insects—and for the largest—wolves and grizzly bears. Their wastes nourish plant growth, and when they die, arctic foxes, jaegers, and other scavengers feast.

Perhaps the most important part-time members of the tundra ecosystem are the birds. Only a few species of birds live here in the winter, but dozens of species crowd the tundra every summer. They link the tundra with ecosystems as close as the Brooks Range and as far away as Antarctica.

When the migratory birds arrive, they transform the tundra, filling the air with their calls and crowding the ponds and meadows. Many species nest in one habitat and search for food in another. Dry ridges, riversides, marshes, ponds, mud flats, and ocean shores are all within easy reach. Without the tundra's crucial nesting grounds, many species of birds would struggle. Some might even become extinct.

(TOP) **GRIZZLY BEARS *(URSUS ARCTOS)***

(BOTTOM) **GRAY WOLF *(CANIS LUPUS)***

MIGRATORY BIRDS

The most important living links between the North Slope tundra ecosystem and other ecosystems around the world are the migratory birds. Millions of birds come to the North Slope every spring. Many build nests and lay eggs even before all the snow has melted. Their eggs hatch in early summer, when the lush plants and hordes of aquatic insects provide ample food for the chicks.

The tundra provides crucial nesting habitat for these species of birds. In turn, the birds provide food for tundra predators and fertilizer for the poor tundra soils. The main groups of migratory birds on the tundra are waterfowl, seabirds, shorebirds, songbirds, and raptors.

**TUNDRA SWAN
(CYGNUS COLUMBIANUS)**

Waterfowl Geese, ducks, loons, and swans are medium-sized to large birds that swim well. Some also dive. Geese eat sedges and other freshwater plants. Ducks eat a wide range of foods. Some feed on aquatic plants, while others catch fish or root around in muddy lakebeds for invertebrates. Some ducks forage only in freshwater, but others feed only in salt water. Loons dive deep into lakes in search of fish and mollusks. Tundra swans are the largest waterfowl on the North Slope. The chicks eat aquatic insects, but adults feed on aquatic plants. Waterfowl nest on the sedge-moss tundra or on bluffs above large rivers.

Seabirds Gulls, terns, and jaegers are medium-sized birds. Their long, narrow wings make them swift, graceful flyers. Some seabirds plunge into the water from high in the air to nab fish. Others skim just above the water and pluck out fish that swim near the surface. Terns eat only fish, but gulls and jaegers also scavenge and feed on rodents, birds, or food they steal from other birds. Seabirds spend most of their lives at sea, but come onto land to build nests and raise their young. They nest on the sedge-moss tundra or on high bluffs overlooking the ocean.

**LONG-TAILED JAEGER
(STERCORARIUS LONGICAUDUS)**

SEMIPALMATED PLOVER
(CHARADRIUS SEMIPALMATUS)

Shorebirds Sandpipers and plovers are small to medium-sized birds with long, thin legs. They forage for insects, mollusks, and crustaceans along the shores of ponds or the ocean. Plovers sometimes stomp on the ground to make invertebrates come to the surface. Most shorebirds nest among the ponds and marshes of the sedge-moss tundra. Others, such as the American golden plover, nest on drier ground in tussock meadows or on high-center polygons.

Songbirds Sparrows, longspurs, snow buntings, and northern wheatears are small birds that eat seeds, berries, or insects—often changing their diet as the seasons change. Most species, including tree sparrows and snow buntings, nest in shrubs in riparian areas. A few songbirds, such as northern wheatears, are more common on tussock tundra. Others, such as Lapland longspurs, nest and forage throughout the tundra.

SNOW BUNTING
(PLECTROPHENAX NIVALIS)

GYRFALCON
(FALCO RUSTICOLUS)

Raptors Falcons, hawks, and eagles are medium-sized to large birds of prey. These carnivores have sharp talons and powerful, hooked bills. Raptors hunt lemmings, voles, siksiks, and smaller birds. They spot their prey while soaring above the tundra or perched on a high place, such as a pingo. Most will also eat scavenged meat. Raptors nest in tall shrubs along rivers, or on the ground on river bluffs or pingos.

The area around Teshekpuk Lake is especially important for migratory birds, even after young birds have left their nests. In late summer, adult geese gather on marshy ground near the lake to go through their annual molt. During this time, they lose their old feathers and grow new ones. While they are molting the birds cannot fly, so they must find an area where they can reach plenty of food by walking or swimming a short distance. The molting area must also be hard for predators to reach. With its wet ground and hundreds of ponds, the area around Teshekpuk Lake is ideal.

After the molt is over, Teshekpuk Lake becomes a staging area—a place where thousands of waterfowl and shorebirds gather before they start their fall migration. When the time comes to head south, the birds rise into the air in waves. Thousands of birds may depart within a few hours, following the same route their ancestors did.

OTHER LINKS BETWEEN ECOSYSTEMS

Birds and other animals may be the most visible link between the North Slope tundra and other ecosystems, but water and air also connect the tundra to the rest of the planet. Water currents in the Arctic Ocean flow past northern Europe, Canada, and Asia before reaching the North Slope. Air currents from other parts of the world also affect the tundra. Whatever goes into the air in Europe and Asia eventually ends up in Alaska's air.

One of the most important ways that arctic tundra helps the global ecosystem is by removing carbon dioxide from the air. In a process called respiration, animals and plants take in oxygen and release carbon dioxide as a waste product. Unlike animals, plants also take in carbon dioxide from the air—much more than they release during respiration. They use it to make carbohydrates during photosynthesis.

When plants die in warmer ecosystems, decomposers break down their carbohydrates and release carbon dioxide back into the atmosphere. But on the arctic tundra, decomposition occurs very slowly. Most dead plant material doesn't decay and produce more carbon dioxide. Instead, dead leaves and stems accumulate as peat. Most of the carbon dioxide that tundra plants take in while they are alive remains locked within peat after the plants die. As a result, the arctic tundra lowers the total amount of carbon dioxide in Earth's atmosphere. The tundra is what scientists call a carbon sink.

Like the North Slope tundra, our whole planet is a mosaic. It is a patchwork of different ecosystems that are linked to one another through the movement of animals, air, and water. Each ecosystem gains something from and contributes something to other ecosystems. Rivers flow from mountains to plains to the sea. Water that evaporates from one ecosystem falls as rain or snow in another. Migratory animals link ecosystems that are thousands of miles apart. Even migrants that live on the North Slope for just a few months of every year contribute to the tundra's biodiversity. Even plant seeds can cross over into other ecosystems, riding in the fur of animals or on the wind.

Just as the loss of one species can severely damage the arctic tundra, the addition of one species can have a big effect too. On the North Slope, the species with the greatest potential to alter the ecosystem is us—human beings.

ON THE TUNDRA, SPHAGNUM MOSS *(SPHAGNUM)* AND OTHER PLANTS DO NOT DECAY AFTER THEY DIE. OVER MANY YEARS, THE PLANTS ACCUMULATE AND FORM PEAT DEPOSITS.

CHAPTER 6

PEOPLE ON ALASKA'S NORTH SLOPE TUNDRA

Humans have been part of the North Slope tundra ecosystem for thousands of years. They came to northern Alaska by walking across the Bering land bridge from Asia, as caribou and other animals once did. Between thirty thousand and ten thousand years ago, several waves of human immigrants traveled over the land bridge.

Most of them moved south, eventually settling throughout North and South America. But some traveled north and east onto the North Slope tundra. Their descendants, the Inupiat and Yup'ik people, still live on the North Slope today.

The first humans on the North Slope were nomads who followed the caribou on their annual migrations. They relied on the herds for meat, clothing, and tools. Later, people settled in permanent villages along the region's rivers. Some hunted caribou in summer and caught fish in spring and fall. Others hunted the bowhead whales that migrated past Point Barrow twice each year. A successful whale hunt brought in enough food to feed a whole village for months. Hunting is still the main source of food for many Alaskans.

In 1741, Russian sailors "discovered" Alaska. Their captain was Vitus Bering,

THESE YUP'IK GIRLS ARE DESCENDANTS OF THE FIRST PEOPLES WHO INHABITED ALASKA'S NORTH SLOPE.

whose name was later given to the sea separating Siberia and Alaska. When Bering's ship wrecked on its way back to Russia, he and many of his crew died. Those who made it home told others about the thousands of fur seals and sea otters they had seen along Alaska's southeast coast. A single pelt, or furred skin, could be sold for more money than most sailors made in a year. Soon more ships headed for Alaska, as men rushed to gather as many furs as they could.

Russia claimed Alaska as its own territory, but did not limit how many seals hunters could kill. Within one hundred years, the Alaskan Fur Rush was over. The seals and other fur-bearing animals had been hunted nearly to extinction.

The Fur Rush was the first of many rushes in Alaska. Others followed the discovery of copper, coal, and gold. In each of these rushes, prospectors came to Alaska just long enough to harvest the resource, and then they moved on. They gave little thought to the health of the land.

In 1867 the United States bought Alaska from Russia for $7.2 million—about two cents per acre (five cents per hectare). Parts of Alaska went through rushes, such as the Gold Rush along the Yukon River from 1896 to 1900, but the North Slope remained almost untouched. It was too hard to reach, either by sea or land. Ships could come to the coast in summer, but in winter, a thick layer of ice covered the ocean. The Brooks Range could be crossed at only a few places, and no roads reached the North Slope.

OIL ON THE NORTH SLOPE

In the early 1920s, geologists found oil seeping out of the ground about

WITHIN ONE HUNDRED YEARS, THE ALASKAN FUR RUSH WAS OVER. THE SEALS AND OTHER FUR-BEARING ANIMALS HAD BEEN HUNTED NEARLY TO EXTINCTION.

50 miles (80 kilometers) southeast of Barrow. In the cool air, the oil congealed into a hard, sticky mass. Local people cut chunks of it to burn in their stoves. Suspecting the ground might hold big deposits of oil, the U.S. government set aside more than half of the North Slope as a potential oil field. This is the area now known as the National Petroleum Reserve-Alaska (NPR-A).

After Alaska became the forty-ninth state in 1959, oil exploration continued across the North Slope. In 1968, geologists found oil on privately-owned land near Prudhoe Bay. This was not just another small strike. With nearly thirteen billion barrels of oil, it was the largest oil reserve ever found in North America.

Because crude oil is used to make gasoline, lubricants, and plastic, harvesting this oil became a high priority for the United States. At the time, most of the nation's gas and oil came from other countries, and gasoline prices were sky-high. Having our own source of oil became very important. The Oil Rush was on.

But transportation on the North Slope was still difficult. To move oil out of Prudhoe Bay, several oil companies worked together to build the Trans-Alaska Pipeline. The pipeline reaches from Prudhoe Bay to Valdez, a town 800 miles (1,300 kilometers) away on Alaska's southern coast. In Valdez, the crude oil is loaded onto ships that take it to refineries in other states.

Developing the oil fields brought billions of dollars into Alaska. The state used its share of the money to build hospitals, schools, and sewer systems. Much of the money was paid to tribal governments for the benefit of the native people.

So far, people involved with the Oil Rush have been more careful about how they treat the land than people involved in earlier rushes. Environmental protection laws require scientific studies of how tundra plants and animals might be affected by oil production. The laws also require oil companies to find ways to reduce their impact on the environment. For example, long stretches of the Trans-Alaska Pipeline were built high enough above the ground to allow caribou and other animals to walk under them. As oil production in the Prudhoe Bay fields geared up, the U.S. government protected part of the tundra ecosystem from industrial use. It set aside an area south and east of Prudhoe Bay as the Arctic National Wildlife Refuge (ANWR).

HUMANS BRING CHANGE

Even with laws to protect the environment, the oil industry has damaged the North Slope tundra. Other kinds of human activity have also harmed the land and its wildlife. The air and water have been polluted, and large chunks of habitat have been destroyed.

Some animals, such as musk oxen, have been overhunted. A few other tundra animals have increased in number as a result of human presence. In the past, ravens flew south for the winter. Now many stay on the tundra in winter, finding shelter near buildings or drill rigs. The number of gulls

and arctic foxes has also increased. These scavengers find easy meals at trash cans and garbage dumps. Having more gulls and foxes on the tundra is not necessarily a good thing. Both species create problems when their populations get too high. They kill large numbers of bird eggs and chicks. Arctic foxes often carry rabies—a deadly disease that can spread to other animals and people that encounter infected foxes.

Another problem that occurs on the tundra is pollution. More than eight hundred oil wells have already been drilled on the North Slope. Even when workers are careful, small amounts of oil spill on the ground. Large spills are always a danger. Chemicals used to keep the machinery running have to be replaced occasionally. In the past, the old chemicals were poured into pits dug in the ground.

(ABOVE) **A NORTH SLOPE OIL FIELD AND DRILLING PLANT**

(LEFT) **SECTIONS OF THE TRANS-ALASKA PIPELINE ARE BUILT FAR ENOUGH OFF THE GROUND FOR ANIMALS TO PASS BENEATH.**

Toxic substances from these pits spread through the surrounding ground.

Tundra habitat suffers another kind of damage from human actions. Roads, buildings, and oil wells all produce heat that penetrates into the ground and melts the upper layer of permafrost. Then the ground turns to muddy slush and sinks several feet. Scientists use the term "thermokarst" to describe the sunken ground. On flat areas, huge, soupy craters open up. Water drains away from ponds. Then the plants and animals that lived in the ponds die.

The problem is even worse on hills, where the warmed, mushy soil slides downhill. Deeper layers of permafrost then become exposed to the Sun and begin to thaw. Over time, more and more layers of permafrost soften and slump downhill. Thermokarst on a tundra hillside can start a process of erosion that goes on for decades.

For many years, people tried to avoid creating thermokarst by not making roads. Instead, they drove directly on the tundra. But that also caused thermokarst, because most tundra plants die if a vehicle drives on them. Even snowmobiles are heavy enough to kill tundra vegetation. When the plants die, they no longer insulate the soil. The permafrost warms up and starts to melt, and the soil sinks. The tracks where the vehicle drove become boggy strips of mud and muck. Tracks that were made by a single vehicle driving over the tundra fifty years ago are still visible today.

Sedge-moss tundra recovers from damage more quickly than tussock tundra, but still needs more than twenty years to bounce back. When plants do return, the new community usually has fewer species than the original one.

LIMITING THE DAMAGE

Because tundra plants recover so slowly, people have looked for less damaging ways to work and travel on the North Slope. The Dalton Highway, which runs parallel to the Trans-Alaska Pipeline, is made of gravel and is several feet thick, so the permafrost beneath it will not warm up and thaw. This highway is still the only road that spans the North Slope from north to south. When oil workers must drive over the roadless tundra, they use large vehicles with huge, puffy tires. These "Rolligons" spread the weight of the vehicle over a wider track, causing less damage to plants.

Another way to protect the fragile ecosystem is to work there only in winter. This may seem like the worst time to be on the tundra, but in winter there's no mud to get stuck in and no mosquitoes to battle. In early winter, oil crews pump water along the routes where roads will be needed. As the water freezes, more is added until a thick layer of ice forms. The resulting ice road is as durable as blacktop. It keeps heat away from the permafrost and protects plants underneath the road from being crushed. In spring, the oil workers leave, the road melts, and life on the tundra continues.

FUTURE OF THE TUNDRA

Ice roads and Rolligons help protect permafrost from the activities of humans on the tundra, but the North Slope ecosystem is also affected by actions that occur far away. Migratory animals need to be safe and able to find food in their winter habitats and along their travel routes. Birds that summer on the North Slope often face water pollution, overhunting, or loss of habitat in their winter homes.

Other threats come from the atmosphere, which links the North Slope to ecosystems all over the world. Global wind patterns sweep air pollution from northern Europe and Asia across Alaska. At times, the pollution is so thick it forms smog called arctic haze. This smog contains toxic pollutants such as zinc, lead, and pesticides. One pesticide, dichloro-diphenyl-trichloroethane (DDT), can devastate bird populations. Female birds exposed to DDT produce eggs with very fragile shells. In many cases, the eggs break and the chicks inside die. The use of DDT was banned in the United States in 1973, but it is still made in the United States and used in other countries.

Another problem that starts far from the tundra is the gradual melting of permafrost due to global warming. Although Earth's climate goes through natural cycles of warming and cooling, most scientists agree that human activities, such as burning fossil fuels, are causing the atmosphere to heat up at an alarming rate. Our cars and industries produce more carbon dioxide and other greenhouse gases than the global ecosystem can handle. As these gases build up in the atmosphere, they trap heat from the Sun, causing the planet's average temperature to rise.

Signs of global warming have already shown up on the North Slope. Compared to a few decades ago, ice cover on ponds forms later in autumn, is thinner all winter long, and breaks up earlier in spring. The tundra's permafrost is slightly warmer now than it was in 1950.

Scientists think that by the year 2100, the average temperature on the North Slope will be 12.6° Fahrenheit (7° Celsius) higher in winter and 5.4° Fahrenheit (3° Celsius) higher in summer than it is now. Such a change would completely alter the tundra ecosystem. Rising seas could cover much of the coastal plain, wiping out the sedge-moss tundra. Already, about 8 feet (more than 2 meters) of sedge-moss tundra washes into the Beaufort Sea every year. Warmer, longer summers could cause permafrost to thaw, creating huge areas

of thermokarst. Boreal forests could colonize land that is now covered by tussock tundra. More species of birds could migrate to the warmer North Slope, where they would compete with the current residents for limited food and nesting sites.

One of the most harmful changes might be a faster rate of decomposition. If decomposers become more active, they will consume tons of tundra peat and release huge amounts of carbon dioxide. Instead of removing carbon dioxide from the air, the tundra would become another source of the greenhouse gas.

It is impossible to predict exactly how global warming could change our planet, but large increases in temperature will probably disrupt the North Slope tundra and many other ecosystems. That's why it makes sense to try to slow down global warming now. Once a big change happens, it may be too late to repair the damage. As scientists have learned by watching a tundra hillside continue to erode fifty years after one car drove across it, the consequences of what we do today can have lasting effects on the natural world.

HULAHULA RIVER VALLEY IN THE ARCTIC NATIONAL WILDLIFE REFUGE, ALASKA

WHAT YOU CAN DO TO HELP

To protect Alaska's North Slope, we must make informed choices about how we will interact with the land and the wildlife in the future. But there are also some things you can do at home to help preserve and protect this very special ecosystem. For example, if enough people reduce their use of oil, gasoline, and natural gas, there will be less pressure to exploit the arctic tundra for oil. At the same time, these efforts will help limit pollution and slow global warming. Here are some tips for conserving energy and preventing pollution.

• Set your thermostat lower in winter and higher in summer.

• Whenever possible, take public transportation, such as buses and subways.

• Learn more about renewable energy sources, such as solar and wind energy. Encourage your representatives in Congress to fund programs that develop renewable energy technology.

• Don't pour household cleaners, paints, oil, or gasoline into sinks, bathtubs, toilets, or onto the ground. They might seep into a groundwater system and pollute it. Contact your city or county government to find out how to dispose of hazardous materials such as these.

• Many of the birds that nest on the North Slope spend winter in the continental United States. You can help them by participating in migratory bird counts and bird-banding projects.

• Use safe alternatives to harsh household cleaners. Instead of commercial window cleaner, try a mixture of vinegar and water. A paste of baking soda and water effectively cleans sinks, tubs, and toilets.

YOU CAN BE INVOLVED IN FUTURE PLANNING

New concerns about how to meet the nation's future oil needs have renewed interest in the oil reserves in northern Alaska. It is probably not realistic to think that oil can be extracted from these areas without damaging the arctic tundra ecosystem.

The land surrounding Teshekpuk Lake and the Colville River delta are likely to be rich in oil, but exploring the area and removing any oil found there would probably have a major impact on migratory birds and caribou. Waterfowl and shorebirds are especially sensitive to industrial activity. Oil companies may also seek out other promising sites in the National Petroleum Reserve-Alaska (NPR-A) and the Arctic National Wildlife Refuge (ANWR). About two-thirds of the North Slope tundra ecosystem lies within these two areas of federally owned land.

Because both the NPR-A and the ANWR are publicly owned, all Americans have a say in what happens in those areas. Any oil development on these lands requires the permission of the government. The agencies that decide whether to allow drilling ask for comments from the public about the proposed activities. Watch for news stories about the tundra and plans to drill for oil and gas in the NPR-A and the ANWR. Find out what measures will be taken to shield the permafrost, guard against pollution, and protect tundra wildlife. Then let the agencies and your elected representatives know your thoughts.

As a society, we need to decide what level of damage is acceptable, and whether some parts of the arctic tundra should not be developed at all. We also need to decide whether to support the development of other kinds of energy, such as solar and wind power, that are less damaging to the environment.

To write to the president:
The President
The White House
Washington, D.C. 20500

To write to senators from your state:
The Honorable (name of your senator)
United States Senate
Washington, D.C. 20510

To write to a representative in Congress:
The Honorable (name of your representative)
U.S. House of Representatives
Washington, D.C. 20515

WEBSITES TO VISIT FOR MORE INFORMATION

Many government agencies, universities, and nonprofit groups have websites where you can learn more about the tundra. A few of them are listed here.

Alyeska Pipeline

<http://www.alyeska-pipe.com>

At this site, you can learn about the group of oil companies that joined forces to build and operate the Trans-Alaska Pipeline.

Arctic National Wildlife Refuge

<http://arctic.fws.gov/arctic.html>

This is the refuge's official site. It was created and is maintained by the U.S. Fish and Wildlife Service.

The Center for Energy Efficiency and Renewable Technologies

<http://www.cleanpower.org>

This website provides information about environmental groups and technology companies working to develop clean, renewable energy resources.

Ducks Unlimited

<http://www.ducks.org>

This website offers information about preserving the habitat of waterfowl and shorebirds throughout North America.

This Arctic Circle

<http://arcticcircle.uconn.edu>

Try this website if you are interested in learning more about the natural resources and human cultures of the Arctic.

The U.S. Bureau of Land Management

<http://wwwndo.ak.blm.gov/npra>

This is the website for the government agency that manages the National Petroleum Reserve-Alaska. Its Environmental Impact Statement on proposed oil development in the NPR-A contains detailed information about the plants and wildlife of the Colville River delta and the Teshekpuk Lake area.

FOR FURTHER READING

Books

Bruemmer, Fred. *Arctic Animals*. Toronto: McClelland and Stewart, 1986.

Burt, Page. *Barrenland Beauties: Showy Plants of the Arctic Coast*. Yellowknife, NWT: Outcrop Publishers, 1991.

Chernov, Yu I. *The Living Tundra*. D. Love, translator. New York: Cambridge University Press, 1985.

Lopez, Barry. *Arctic Dreams: Imagination and Desire in a Northern Landscape*. New York: Charles Scribner's Sons, 1986.

McPhee, John. *Coming into the Country*. New York: Bantam Books, 1976.

Mech, David L., Michael K. Phillips, and Roger A. Caras. *The Arctic Wolf: Ten Years With the Pack*. Stillwater, MN: Voyageur Press, 1997.

Miller, Debbie S., and Margaret Murie. *Midnight Wilderness: Journeys in Alaska's Arctic National Wildlife Refuge*. Portland, OR: Alaska Northwest Books, 2000.

Patent, Dorothy Hinshaw. *Biodiversity*. New York: Clarion Books, 1996.

Pielou, E. C. *A Naturalist's Guide to the Arctic*. Chicago: The University of Chicago Press, 1994.

Scott, Michael. *Ecology*. New York: Oxford University Press, 1995.

Soper, Tony. *The Arctic: A Guide to Coastal Wildlife*. Guilford, CT: The Globe Pequot Press, 2001.

Stonehouse, Bernard. *Animals of the Arctic: The Ecology of the Far North*. New York: Henry Holt, 1971.

Whitman, Sylvia. *This Land Is Your Land: The American Conservation Movement*. Minneapolis: Lerner Publications Company, 1994.

Magazine Articles

Bruemmer, Fred. "Life upon the Permafrost." *Natural History*, April 1987.

Heinrich, Bernd. "The Antifreeze of Bees." *Natural History*, July 1990.

Kukal, Olga. "Caterpillars on Ice." *Natural History*, January 1988.

GLOSSARY

active layer: the portion of the soil that is free of ice in summer

alga (pl. algae): a kind of primary producer, usually living in water; may have one cell or many cells

alpine tundra: an area on high mountains where only short plants grow

Arctic Circle: imaginary line around the northern third of Earth, marking the northernmost appearance of the Sun on December 22 each year

arctic haze: smog over arctic areas

arctic tundra: the area north of the Arctic Circle where only short plants grow and deep layers of soil are permanently frozen

bacteria: microscopic, single-celled organisms that lack cell nuclei

biodiversity: the variety of living things found in an ecosystem

carbon sink: an ecosystem that takes in more carbon dioxide than it releases into the atmosphere

carnivore: an animal that eats other animals

colony: a group of animals of the same species that live close to one another

crustacean: a member of the group of animals, closely related to insects, with a segmented body and an outer covering or shell. Crabs and crayfish are crustaceans.

deciduous: having leaves that fall off at a certain season of the year

decomposer: an organism that gains nourishment from dead organisms or waste materials of other organisms and recycles the nutrients they contain

delta: a broad area where a river spreads out as it flows into a lake or ocean

dormant: inactive for a long period of time or during a certain season, such as winter

ecosystem: the network of living things in a specific area and the physical factors that support them or limit them

erode: to wear away, usually over a long period of time

forb: a plant, such as a wildflower, that has no woody parts

fungus: an organism that does not perform photosynthesis and must absorb nutrients through its cell walls

global warming: the increase in the average temperature of Earth's atmosphere due to the accumulation of greenhouse gases

greenhouse gas: a gas, such as carbon dioxide, that is produced by burning fossil fuels and that contributes to global warming

habitat: the kind of environment in which a plant or animal normally lives

herbivore: an animal that eats plant material such as leaves, seeds, or nectar

ice wedge: a wall of ice, narrow at the bottom and broad at the top, that develops when water freezes inside a crack in the arctic soil

larva (pl. larvae): an early stage of development in the life of many kinds of animals. In insects, it refers to the young of species that undergo complete metamorphosis (egg, larva, pupa, adult).

lichen: an organism made up of a fungus and an alga that form a single structure

mollusk: a member of the group of animals with soft bodies and hard outer shells. Clams and snails are mollusks.

molt: to shed an outer covering, such as feathers

opportunist: an animal that will eat whatever kind of food is available

patterned ground: a large area of land where repeated freezing and thawing has created cracked patterns in the soil

peat: dead, undecayed plant material, often densely packed

permafrost: the portion of the ground that stays frozen year round

photosynthesis: the process by which plants and other primary producers harness solar energy and produce carbohydrates

pingo: a cone-shaped hill with a core of ice, formed by repeated freezing and thawing of ground

pollen: a powdery substance made by flowers to carry sperm, or male sex cells

pollinate: to transfer pollen to the female parts of a flower so fertilization can occur

polygon: any shape with many sides; on the arctic tundra, a many-sided patch of patterned ground surrounded by ice wedges

precipitation: rain, snow, or other forms of moisture that fall from the sky

primary consumer: an animal that eats primary producers

primary producer: an organism that makes its own food through photosynthesis

respiration: the process by which organisms take in oxygen and give off carbon dioxide

riparian: along a river or stream

scavenger: an animal that eats meat it finds rather than animals it has killed

secondary consumer: an animal that eats other animals; a carnivore

sedge-moss tundra: an area of arctic tundra where mosses and water sedges are the dominant plants

staging area: a place where migratory birds gather before beginning their migration

thermokarst: slumping ground that occurs when permafrost thaws

tundra: a kind of ecosystem in cold or high-altitude areas where only short vegetation grows

tussock: a clump of vegetation; on the arctic tundra, each tussock is made of the leaves and stems of one plant of the sedge *Eriophorum vaginatum*

tussock tundra: an area of arctic tundra where tussock sedges are the dominant plant

wetland: an area that is flooded for all or part of the year

zooplankton: one of the many tiny, often microscopic, animals that live in water and are an important source of food for secondary consumers

INDEX

ABOUT THE AUTHOR

Cherie Winner is a biologist, teacher, writer, and photographer. In 1996 she survived three months of winter in Canada's Yukon Territory, where she lived in a cabin in the woods, wrote a book about trout, observed wolves at play, and dreamed of warmer places. She has a Ph.D. in zoology, has taught classes at the university level, and has written nine other nature books for young readers. Four of her books have been named Outstanding Science Trade Books by the Children's Book Council and National Science Teachers Association. Ms. Winner lives in western Colorado with her dog Sheba, who found the Yukon much too cold for comfort, and her cat Smudge, who is glad she didn't make that trip.

PHOTO ACKNOWLEDGEMENTS

The photographs in this book are reproduced courtesy of, © Joe McDonald/Visuals Unlimited, pp. 2–3, 15, 18 (right), 36 (left), 53 (bottom); © Charles McRae/Visuals Unlimited, pp. 9, 63; © Arthur Morris/Visuals Unlimited, pp. 12, 23 (bottom); © Mark Newman/Visuals Unlimited, p. 14 (top); © Gary Schultz, pp. 14 (bottom), 37; © H.S. Rose/Visuals Unlimited, pp. 16, 51 (bottom); © Patrick J. Endres/Visuals Unlimited, pp. 18 (left), 51 (top); © Tom J. Ulrich/Visuals Unlimited, p. 20; Jamie Berger, University of Alaska-Fairbanks, p. 21 (left); © Beth Davidow/Visuals Unlimited, pp. 21 (right), 23 (top left); © John Gerlach/Visuals Unlimited, p. 23 (top right); © Hugh Rose/Visuals Unlimited, p. 24 (top); © Rick and Nora Bowers/Visuals Unlimited, p. 24 (bottom); © Steve McCutcheon/Visuals Unlimited, pp. 27, 55, 56, 59 (right); © Kim Francisco/Visuals Unlimited, p. 28; © George Herben Photo/Visuals Unlimited, p. 33; © Dan Guravich/CORBIS, p. 34; © Glenn M. Oliver/Visuals Unlimited, p. 36 (right); © Tom Bean/CORBIS, p. 39; © Tom Walker/Visuals Unlimited, pp. 43, 44 (right); © Gil Lopez-Espina/Visuals Unlimited, p. 44 (left); © Scott T. Smith/CORBIS, p. 47; © Maslowski/Visuals Unlimited, p. 52 (top); © Darrell Gulin/CORBIS, p. 52 (bottom); © Kennan Ward/CORBIS, p. 53 (top); © Steve Kaufman/CORBIS, p. 53 (center); Adam Lerner/IPS, p. 59 (left). Maps and illustrations on pp. 8, 11, 30–31 by Bill Hauser. Bottom border by CORBIS Royalty Free Images. Cover image: Joe McDonald/Visuals Unlimited.